Hajime
in the
North Woods

Text and Illustrations by
Kazumi Inose Wilds

Arcade Publishing • New York

On a cold winter's day in the North Country, a
little boy was born. Outside, the snow drifted
and the wind blew. Inside, his papa and mama
were smiling and their hearts were warm. They
were happy to have such a beautiful boy. They
named him Hajime.

When the snow began to melt, his mama took him outside. Hajime could hear the birds and chipmunks and squirrels chatter to each other. The wind whispered that spring was on its way.

"It's coming! It's coming," the birds repeated.

A squirrel poked his face from around a tree.

"Hello, Hajime," he said. "The animals in the North Woods want to meet you!"

"The North Woods!" said Hajime to his mama, his eyes wide with excitement. His mother smiled. She didn't understand what little Hajime was telling her.

The days grew warmer. One night when the moon was full, Hajime woke to the sound of tapping at his window. He saw two raccoons.

   "Wake up, wake up!" they said. "It's time to go to the North Woods. The animals are waiting."

   "I'm ready!" said Hajime.

One raccoon took Hajime on his back, and off
they ran. They passed through woods where
owls hooted and baby rabbits slept.

They traveled for a long time along the shores of lakes where fish swam and loons nested. At last they reached the deepest part of the North Woods.

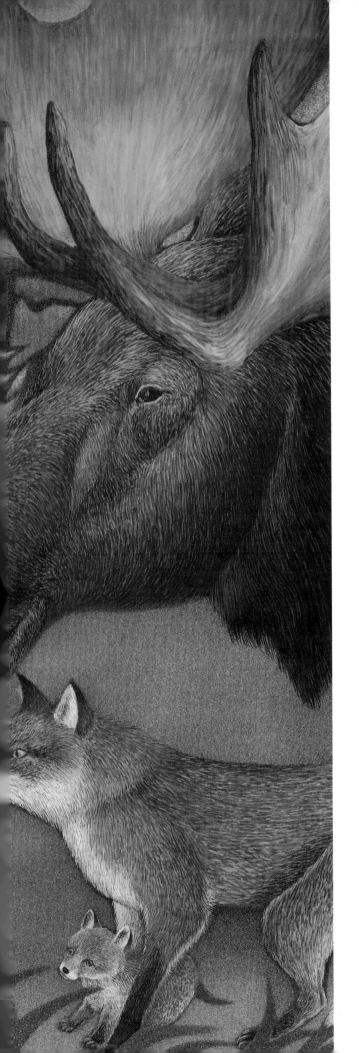

The animals were waiting for him.

"Hello, Hajime! We're glad you've come!"

"Welcome to the North Woods," said Big King Moose in his deep voice. "We know you're a good boy."

"Thank you for inviting me!" Hajime replied happily.

He played and laughed all night long with his
new friends.
    "Would you like to stay and live with us here
in the North Woods?" asked Black Bear.
    "Oh, yes!" exclaimed Hajime.

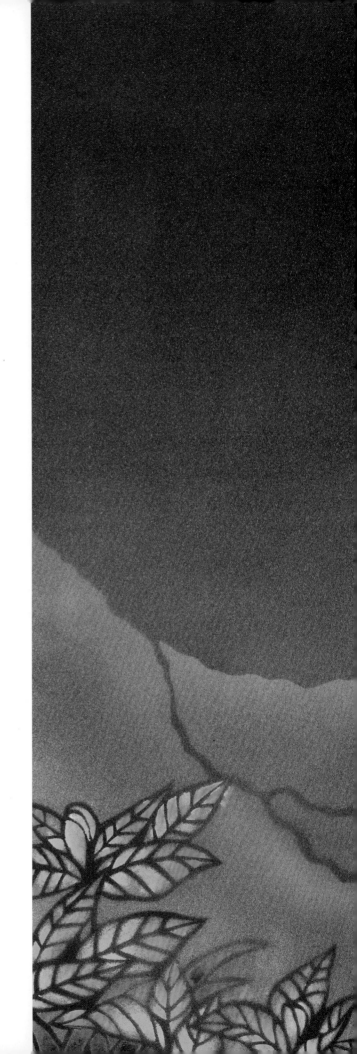

"But what about Papa and
Mama?" he wondered.

"They don't understand us,"
said Big King Moose. "Only babies
do. Grown-ups lose our language
and forget they knew us. They
hunt, and chop down the forest."

"But Mama loves animals.
And Papa loves trees."

The animals murmured
among themselves. Black Bear
shook his large head slowly.

"Stay with us, Hajime," he
said. "Don't go back to the
grown-ups."

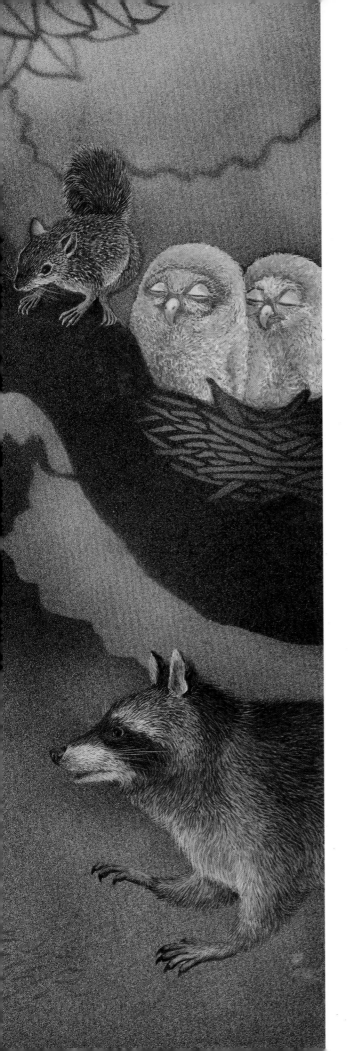

Hajime suddenly felt very lonely. He wished he could see his papa's face. He missed his mama. He was getting very hungry. He . . .

MAAMAAAAAAA!"

I never heard a louder baby!" said the turtle,
pulling into his shell.

"I can't stand it! Not one more minute!"
said the beaver, diving into the pond.

Even the raccoons were startled.

"Take him back to his mama and papa,"
said Big King Moose to Gray Wolf with a sigh.

Gray Wolf, the Great Runner of the Forest,
took Hajime on his back and raced like the wind.

Hurry, Gray Wolf! Dawn is coming!"

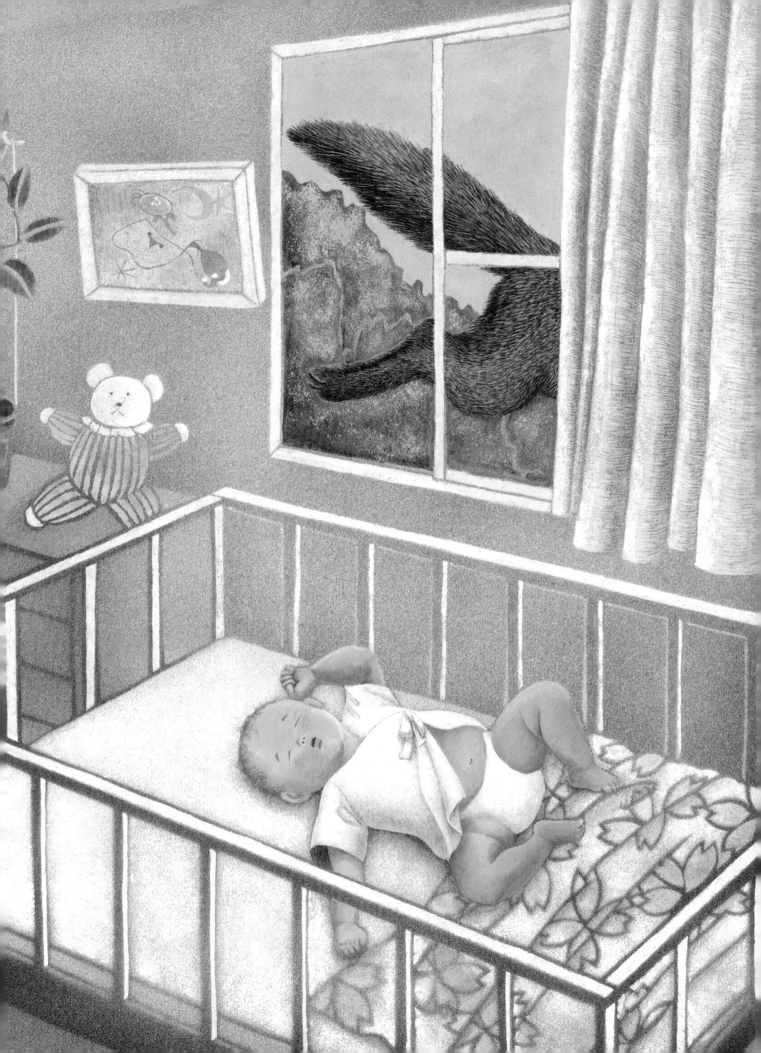

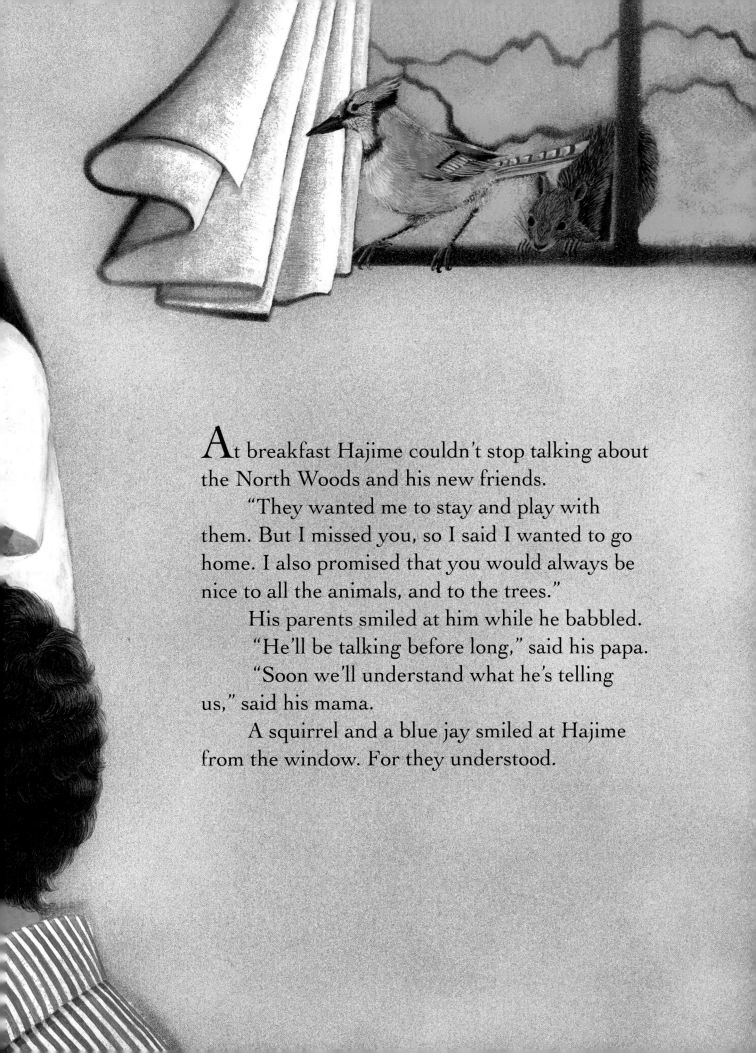

At breakfast Hajime couldn't stop talking about the North Woods and his new friends.

"They wanted me to stay and play with them. But I missed you, so I said I wanted to go home. I also promised that you would always be nice to all the animals, and to the trees."

His parents smiled at him while he babbled.

"He'll be talking before long," said his papa.

"Soon we'll understand what he's telling us," said his mama.

A squirrel and a blue jay smiled at Hajime from the window. For they understood.

*For Hajime and
the animals I met in the
North Woods*

First Edition

ISBN 1-55970-240-0
Library of Congress Catalog Card
Number 93-34689
Library of Congress
Cataloging-in-Publication
information is available.

Published in the United States by
Arcade Publishing, Inc., New York

Distributed by Little, Brown and
Company

10 9 8 7 6 5 4 3 2 1

Designed by Abby Kagan

IMAGO

Printed in China